HOMESLICE

ADVANCE PRAISE

"Dayton J. Shafer's poetry chapbook *Homeslice* is a phenomenal, poignant debut about a young man and nation coming of age at the turn of the 21st century. Daring, delightful, and brave, *Homeslice* conjures an atmosphere of communal call-and-response, and invites the reader to participate with the provocation, 'Is Your American Dream—?' With tenderness and vulnerability, Shafer glides beneath the smooth allure of the American Dream to confront 'those first tastes of life & death,' racism, othering, consent, misogyny, and gun violence that map the speaker's kaleidoscopic childhood. *Homeslice* charts how the hopeful, cool, and impossibly edgy '90s give way to the tumultuous, violent, and isolating traumas of the 21st century. But despite coming of age in a culture borne of desperation and fear, the speaker demonstrates an avid curiosity about the world, oneself, and the imagination of others. The poems in *Homeslice* blossom with 'the first inklings of other worlds' and celebrate 'an imagination-first life.' Creativity, introspection, and 'say[ing] the unsayable' are the hallmarks of Shafer's luminous power as a writer. And *Homeslice* is a superb example of the avant-garde confronting 'unprocessed trauma.' As a poet, Shafer is unafraid to break the fourth wall. His writing is curiosity-filled, propulsive, and startling as *Homeslice* inspires new human connection and new stories to be told while the American canon shifts again."

—Rita Banerjee, author of *Echo in Four Beats*, *A Night with Kali*, and *Credo: An Anthology of Manifestos and Sourcebook for Creative Writing*

"*Homeslice* unabashedly interrogates and delights in the hardest issues of our nation—race, class, sexuality, violence, familial and communal trauma. Shafer is honest about his own culpability, but these soliloquies are never dour. Instead, they are lit through with humor, joy, horror, sorrow, and empathy. His is a most magnificent, most distinctly American voice."

—Erin Stalcup, author of *Keen*

"In this surprisingly expansive chapbook, Dayton J. Shafer moves swiftly and adeptly through his childhood, masterfully conjuring both the specific and universal in equal measures in this American contemporary-coming-of-age story."
—Caitlin Leffel, senior editor at Union Square & Co.

"These philosophical passages do not shy away from shame, embarrassment, discomfort. These lines probe at big questions—race, class, puberty, family, violence—with equal parts dark nostalgia and humor. I felt moved, alternately, to laugh aloud and choke back the tears of recognition. This manuscript reveals the true experience of being an American: simultaneously embracing and rejecting one's identity at every turn."
—Frances Cannon, author of *Walter Benjamin Reimagined: A Graphic Translation of Poetry, Prose, Aphorisms, and Dreams*

HOMESLICE

Monologues of
Millennialhood

DAYTON J. SHAFER

Alternating Current Press
Boulder, Colorado

Copyright © 2023 Dayton J. Shafer
All rights reserved

Published by Alternating Current Press
Boulder, Colorado 80302
altcurrentpress.com
All rights reserved

Library of Congress Control Number: 2023943667
ISBN-13 (paperback): 978-1-946580-37-5
ISBN-10 (paperback): 1-946580-37-6
ISBN-13 (ebook): 978-1-946580-38-2

Interior and cover design: Leah Angstman
Author photo: Jess Dewes © 2023
Interior illustration: Josie Colt © 2023

The following is a work of imagination created by the author. All names, individuals, places, items, brands, events, characters, &c., are the product of the author's imagination, are used fictitiously, or are entirely coincidental.

No part of this publication may be reproduced, stored in a retrieval system, or transmitted, in any form or by any means, electronic, mechanical, photocopied, recorded, or otherwise, without the prior permission of Alternating Current Press, except for the quotation of brief passages used inside of an article, criticism, or review.

Printed in the United States of America

10 9 8 7 6 5 4 3 2 1

TABLE OF CONTENTS

American Monologue I: Color 15

American Monologue II: Kicking & cannibalism . . 18

American Monologue III: Repression 22

American Monologue IV: Displaced 25

American Monologue V: Desire 29

American Monologue VI: Conservation 34

American Monologue VII: Imagination-first 37

American Monologue VIII: Gantlet 42

American Monologue IX: Greater good 47

American Monologue X: Communal trauma 52

For the Field ... always.

These are nonfiction composite characterization monologues—multiple voices of data melded and arranged together by similar themes, stories, motifs, or events. *Homeslice* was originally written as a theatrical piece. Notes for casting and staging can be found in the end pages.

American Monologue I:

COLOR

IS YOUR AMERICAN DREAM
being mesmerized by your friend's dad on his prayer rug?

Whenever you overheard him call you *Little White Devil*, your idea was Taz from *Looney Tunes*, not that when he saw your face, he felt the spit on his face & noose around his neck. You only knew his son was black as the puddles you played in, black as your kindergarten teacher's hand tracing yours through shaving cream tabletops. You never understood their dark skin was disparaged skin. Your parents said, *Skin is skin*, which evolved to *Assholes are assholes*. Skin is skin when you're climbing trees & cutting grass together. Poor is poor when you're both drug mules for the neighborhood basketball court. Money is money when getting off on itchy finger secrets. One day, you guys found scraps of wood behind the flea market & built a candy shop. Coming back a few days later, a naked homeless man was bundled in a corner. He sat upright & pointed at a coiled pile of shit beside him, laying claim to your hard work. Both of you walked to the side & kicked at the creaky wall until it fell on the squatter, your black & white squeals smacking his naked body as he chased you down the alley, never catching up.

IS YOUR AMERICAN DREAM ghetto grown?

American Monologue II:

KICKING &
CANNIBALISM

IS YOUR AMERICAN DREAM rowdy ears on your aunt's pregnant belly as she cooked Thanksgiving potatoes & you cooed to an unborn cousin?

You were the youngest grandchild at that point & wanted more than anything to be higher up in the pecking order. Not out of envy, but camaraderie. A little one to look after. After all four cousins were born, you'd lie underneath the spinal laundry chute that ran the height of the three stories & drop the dirty musk of your family on one another. Around the same time, your dog had eleven puppies. They just kept coming, but when the violet sacks of puppy finally stopped slip-sliding out of her, number eleven didn't move. You rubbed your pooch as she nudged number eleven, & then she spared no hesitation in devouring her dead child. When people began dying, you never cried—only thought of those first tastes of life & death—those reoccurring images of your cousin kicking at life & your cannibalistic dog blocking out the current death of a teammate from bone cancer or cousin from muscular dystrophy. Your dad usually told you & never used coded language, curtly informing you how a granddad died when a tractor rolled over him or of his friend's suicide when you asked why you never went to his house anymore. It's so easy to idolize the people that die when you're young—you never really knew them, saw faults & flaws, true colors when you're both finally adults. The last one to hit you hard was an aunt who knew she was going. Out of the blue, she began writing you these confessional letters, creative marvels she never shared: inken horses & rivers across the margins, these beautiful rolling monologues about her long-dead husband & a whole page devoted to the militaristic preparation of her deviled eggs.

IS YOUR AMERICAN DREAM
new unknowns?

American Monologue III:

REPRESSION

IS YOUR AMERICAN DREAM

your dad carrying his guns to the van & shouting nonsense?

You were seven, & it was the first time you tried to stop the fight. *People fight.* That's all you ever heard. You'd roll up the silken blanket corners & stuff them into your ears & nose—anything to keep out the swift steps & steep voices. They'd usually disperse to their finished attic, but this night, it was full-blow in the middle of the living room. The pitch was never this high. The initial cause has been lost to memory, but as your dad carried his guns to his van, you remember grabbing at him & then him walking right through you, the heavy weight of a rifle knocking you aside, & then you going to your room & picking up your goldfish, squeezing him, telling him not to leave—his eyes bulging, gills slowing until you put him back, until he caught water again & you kissed the bowl over & over, & over again, asking for forgiveness.

IS YOUR AMERICAN DREAM
finding the first cracks?

American Monologue IV:
DiSPLACED

IS YOUR AMERICAN DREAM trading unconscious Christianity for Catholicism?

Not a single face of color amongst your new 1st-grade private school classmates or teachers. Your small city was the first ever to elect a black mayor, but the racial & income inequality was still divided into directional quadrants. You lived in the deep southern side, the diverse side, the poor side, even though the school itself was only a few miles away. Every now & then, there were these sporadic non-white students who would show up. The school would try them out for half a year, but then they'd just disappear. The Sisters wouldn't even bother to address them leaving, just a simple, *They won't be with us anymore*. One of them was your first taste of envy & anger at a race. Spoke Spanish. Superb at every sport. You easily became displaced as the favorite. There was always an understanding, a coupling between your mind & body—hanging from high oaks & leaping to the roof of your shed, the fear of falling was never there, but this was a different type of fall—jealousy for the wrong reasons. The first stab of introspection, the first taste of self-image. For eight years, what made a man was the bantering, the cracks, a brain. Where you grew up the physical was usual: every moment was spent with our bodies climbing trees, wrestling, flexing & punching—everyone had a body; not everyone had a brain. But the first taste of jealousy was different—he had more brains, more body. It became impossible to process male jealousy without violence. Problem being, you were a slight kid—you'd lose, & you knew it. Bigotry took its place. Anger is insatiable & differences are ripe fruit. Horrible thoughts & worse words you planned to say. But then he was gone one morning. Just another, *They won't be with us anymore.*

IS YOUR AMERICAN DREAM
binding, building a self?

American Monologue V:

IS YOUR AMERICAN DREAM

the dying days of an old-world market?

You always went with your mother, & she encouraged curiosity, free rein to leave her side & explore. You'd sit on cold stone floors full of sawdust & soot & graze your fingertips along the burn of comic book edges. Walk through blue rows of triple-stacked aquariums with massive catfish. Follow the leathersmith's polish deepening a set of horse reins. Gaze up at the raised counter where thick-necked deli clerks shouted & tossed paper packages. This time around, you spent your allowance on a jar of bread & butter pickles & sat at the jazz tables in the heart of the market. An old woman plunked down one table over & carefully unfolded a crisp package—she stiffened, stood, sat, marveled at her charming wad of beef. You leaned in, popped the top off your pickles, all the while feeling her eyes on you. So, you walked over, like all kids do, with both hands. An offering, kinship—you not yet ten & a strange woman inhaling a wad of beef in the busy heart of a dying marketplace. She hooked a disc of pickle. You drank the juice & spotted your mom chatting with a friend she grew up with. There is nothing so unsettling & beautiful as the joy on a parent's face when you're not around. You saw your mother move in new ways. You sidled up beside her, still young enough to be at her hip, & watched their happy hands fly back & forth, a rapid blur that could have flowed seamlessly into the rhythm of playground clapping games. You offered a pickle to the friend. She accepted, but only if you took a handful of chewy peppermint. She leaned down, & much too young even to know what was happening, you found yourself looking down her blouse. Can only remember a striking blur—black-earth curls, her vanilla wafting through the marketplace—but something just took you & you reached out, grabbed her breast & shimmied it, hard. Having been here before, she gently took your hand away, *We don't do that just yet*. They laughed about it, but as you left, your mother took you aside & made you understand. Asked if you did it before. You shook your head, & she gently let you know that girls have to be okay with it. How touch was life. How touch was everything. She pointed at the rancid deli clerk, *Do you want him to touch you?* It only took one analogy for the idea of consent to stick & stay. This was how you thought, & after your mother's words, this was now the way of the world. She gave you exploration & empathy, loosened your mind, built your stilts, made you a listener & watcher, alley cat, someone who knows poise, but also when to run alongside wild dogs.

IS YOUR AMERICAN DREAM
the best of both worlds?

American Monologue VI:
CONSERVATION

IS YOUR AMERICAN DREAM

a bloated grate of garbage?

The trash-laden creek bouncing from oil drum to shopping cart to silky pools. Dipping two fingers, skimming the surface of sludge & sewage, going for it—dipping your ankle into the cold creek through broken bottles & chicken buckets stuck on sandstone & studded posts. Trekking upstream to a lagoon of bread bags whistling on debris, & even at ten years old, when your mind was nothing but video games & dog wrestling, you knew this was a problem—the garbage at every oxbow was not right. You went back & told your granny about it. She got real quiet, then blew two streams of smoke from her nose, a queen dragon muttering in her lovely drawl, *Shame ... shame*. You told her you'd take care of it & dove upstream with a canvas bag, pulling out every piece of litter until you walked so far up, the hum of the National Road faded. Until you took a turn to an embankment that rose twelve feet, & underneath, in an earthen root cave, sat a homeless elderly couple, tattered, wide-eyed with shame, backing into the damp recesses of the embankment, & you, ten years old, held out a canvas bag & just said, *Cleaning up the creek*, & how that seemed to calm them, brought them back with sopping wads of garbage bags & broken tchotchkes, fistfuls of fellowship.

IS YOUR AMERICAN DREAM
the dread of shame?

American Monologue VII:

IMAGINATION-FIRST

IS YOUR AMERICAN DREAM
time with Dad on his days off?

It never mattered where you ended up. Sitting on couches or in cars. Curbs or diners. Or, hopefully, the house with jagged rooms. The house where you'd climb on indoor boulders. Find hidden doors to the overgrown courtyard. Reach up long hallways to tap funky sconces creeping down the walls. A unique place that even your young mind could understand as being singular. Sharp corridors. Comforting nooks with knee-high bookcases. Fractured sunlight splashing you from the stained-glass skylight. It wasn't until you were older that you realized the luck, the gravity, the significance that it was a rundown Frank Lloyd Wright house. Your dad &

his friend would disappear into the labyrinth & let you do your thing. Those moments of freedom & trust in a wondrous house, along with being the youngest of four, built your imagination-first life. Even though you loved neighborhood Nerf battles & afterschool theater & life-affirming kickball, the times with just you & your mind in the house of a genius were the first inklings of other worlds. That's when you began writing stories about a brother duo who went on missions to save the world. You loved the way the rhyming lapped off your tongue. How, when you shared them in class, even the nuns laughed, & it was then you saw the light in an imagination-first life. Began collaborating with your best friend on a crime-fighting superhero who was overweight & powerful. Your best friend was overweight & teased incessantly—both of you the worst bullies. But cruelty, self-inflicted or not, was never spoken of. You were short & rude. He was fat & weird. You were perfect together—wrote & illustrated elaborate tales of an overweight & self-conscious superhero who defeated villains using sophisticated blubber-based technology. Took the insults of fat-shaming, the fat, & made it into weapons, into a mask-wearing form of love & grace. Creativity without being led—art not coming from an assignment, but your own minds in the corners of the blacktop & cafegymatorium. The Sisters stopped it, but blasphemy only enticed you more, made you want to explore more, led you to an imagination-first life—the fire that burns when told you can't do something.

IS YOUR AMERICAN DREAM
fighting for a creative life?

American Monologue VIII:

GANTLET

IS YOUR AMERICAN DREAM
the empty-headed glory of youth?

You can't recall a single unselfish thought as a pubescent but do have visceral reactions to reveling in the filth of your football-practice body in the backseat of your brother's car listening to *ATLiens* by OutKast with his girlfriend riding shotgun & the '90s bass shaking your body to bits from the innovative/jankety household speaker your brother installed as a subwoofer. You always peacocked when walking into public places in uniform: loved the, you know, the nods & the questions about the team, spoke of plays & not the team because, in four years, you guys never won a single game. But it never mattered because it was all about that public aura, the bloody uniform & gladiatorial life that the coaches pounded into our young heads. When junior high hit, it wasn't about fun & games anymore, it was just that you played … ahh, that the locker room & the huddle replaced all other sacred spaces, you know, color lines & cruelty, really, peer pressure & puberty changing the air. One of the most offensive environments will always be a locker room full of 8th-grade boys dropping the worst possible racism & rape jokes. I mean … we didn't understand half of what we said, but it was just that we could now say it. We could finally say it. Say the unsayable. That was how we dealt with the dynamics from home & life shifting with every hit on the field or crack in the locker room. We just hoped that we nodded at the right thing, knew the right reference, banished the right losers, survived the gantlet of putting thirty pubescent boys in armor & telling their raging minds to *HIT! HIT! HIT HARDER!* Fifteen years later, you ran into a former teammate for the first time since that 8th-grade season. You guys drank & recollected, I mean you laughed deep, you laughed true about your antics until the racism & rape jokes came up, then your black teammate got real quiet, eased forward, & burst out with a rapid confessional: *I laughed at all those lynching jokes, too! I said all that shit without even thinking.* Kept going & going & going, & then he just chortled, stopped, just this loud piercing, *Hayahh!* You wanted to say something. You did, but just … but there's—I mean … what could you say? What could you say?

Fifteen years later. What could you say? Until he finally said something, in that incredibly awkward silence. *Come on, man ... you were Catholic once, too ... self-love & hate ... that's always going to be our thing.*

IS YOUR AMERICAN DREAM
guarded guilt?

American Monologue IX:

GREATER GOOD

IS YOUR AMERICAN DREAM
finding imagination-first stories in your granny's city barn?

Finished with yard work, you dug deep into this far corner & found a pile of broken machines. Cast-iron stoves & computers. Piles of spiny wires & motherboards spilling from the mouth of an oven. This weird, broke-down vulnerability ... it almost felt like nakedness, like you walked in on someone wiping himself. The shock of it all made you back into a corner & knock over a cart of wastebaskets, & when you grabbed them from hopping up & down, this horror-movie sound scraped the far floor. It came from this corner, this trapped corner between the dead machines & a '40s ice cream truck. You bent

& picked up this random chunk of water heater & hopped onto a suitcase, waiting for some crazy movie-shit violence. But you only saw ears, & then a tubular neck twisting about—going belly-down, the broken slats where the small deer got in. You sat up, stood, sat again, tested the boundaries with how close you could get. He was floating, softly from hoof to hoof, but he saw you, saw each other—he could have left, but didn't. You crab-crawled within a meter & rose, both of you struck, more amazement than fear, a boy & buck in a city barn, & as you reached into his heavy breath, inches away, the young deer nimbly bounded back through the hole in the barn wall. You plunked down & thought of this picture of your young mother hand-feeding a deer at the roadside

—always want to think of your young parents that way—floating along, feeding their wild spirits. You ran to the porch knowing that your granny liked to watch the game & follow up with a smoke & porch swing. You found her & threw all your dramatic flair into picking up the slice of metal & how you thought you'd have to kill something, how you almost touched the young buck, hand to breath, almost got to rub antlers, when your proper Appalachian grandmother nodded at a group of neighbors across the street, *You should talk to that pretty blond one. ... You think she's pretty?* Stunted by the non sequitur, you nodded vigorously. She stabbed her smoking hand at the girl, *Go tell her. Go say that.* You saw the desperation in her eyes, the same way she looked at you after your plays—to her, your flamboyant storytelling actor-self was gay. She took your hand & squeezed it as you kicked the swing into a rhythm. *Don't worry. ... I like the ladies, Granny.* Her rare smile rose. You wish your young self had the words for fluidity, exploration, living for minuscule pockets of passion like with the deer, but you only mumbled something about having a crush on a different girl, which was true, but still felt like a lie.

IS YOUR AMERICAN DREAM
selfless?

American Monologue X:

COMMUNAL TRAUMA

IS YOUR AMERICAN DREAM watching downtown Oklahoma City crumble?

Rage monster when cartoons were cut short by a pile of rubble, you grabbed a handful of grapes & flung them at the TV with a raw throat of bronchitis while screeching about the healing power of Hanna-Barbera. Then the roasted nursery sets came out. Small bodies. The net was just beginning in 1995, & TV news was cresting (mid-O. J. trial) with every network thrusting unfiltered bits of bodies into your sightline. Old enough to stay home when sick, there was no one to process with. Processing. You write the word now & can only think of one thing: the firefighter with the dead infant. You didn't know a soul there, 870 miles away, twenty-eight years ago, but the heat still cranks your chest. You remember snapping up from your sickness, feeling woozy but willing, learning the first lesson of communal trauma: that it can come secondhand. At eleven, it was confusion & anger—walking around the living room & punching cushions. At thirty-nine, it's mostly the same, but with analytics—reading about the misguided motives of the murderers & getting more angry. Frustration at us. Questioning why it took so long to talk openly about our instabilities. There's a video of McVeigh at Waco, two years before the OKC bombing, selling bumper stickers with swastikas & anti-government slogans. It's disgusting as it sounds, beyond chilling, & although his delusion is there, it's his righteousness that rings—a disgruntled soldier, a former shill of American exceptionalism now biting the hand of the master. We mourned for OKC, but still saw the act as another aberration, something few & far between.

Four years later, two teenagers changed all that. The principal harshly came over the intercom & dismissed all of you to the gym for an assembly. Everyone just assumed it was another community death—we had so many—but then nothing, just waiting. Waiting & waiting, with no one saying anything. There was never waiting—every minute of the school day was clocked, written in stone, so this, this was efficiency breaking down—no answers, teachers only scuttling around, fidgeting with their mouths & casting side-eye glances just to make sure no one left. Suddenly, an office worker rammed through the double doors & frantically scanned the crowd—knowing the ritual, she counted & nodded, rushed to your section until her daughter waved her down. They were only a few rows over, & although the words are lost to memory, you definitely remember the mother's shaking panic & the daughter's shaking embarrassment, & then the tiny mother ripping the purse off her daughter's lap & taking off in a dead sprint—how that tactic was genius as the daughter had no choice but to trail after her rattled mother. That's when everyone realized this was no longer a community death or drug bust or someone breaking into cars—an adult did something irrational in public. Whatever happened was about to change the canon. The dean came in & quietly told you in his calming cadence that you'd be dismissed to homeroom & that the school day was over. Every question tossed at every authority figure, but all you got was, *Go home Go home Go home*. A good friend & you were celebrating the half-day by getting high in a state park when a young ranger, no older than twenty-five, crashed through the brambles & told you that two kids slaughtered ten other kids in a school in Colorado & that you needed to go home. He nodded at your blunt & shook his head. *Drink some water first*. Mental health came to the forefront. Mallrat times became something else. Corruption & cause. Many fingers in many different directions. Nine Inch Nails & Marilyn Manson. Violent music & video games. Trench coats. Spiked jewelry. A month later, you & a friend were smoking outside a local coffee shop when a couple of strangers came up & asked about his "Beautiful People" shirt. Your peaceful friend answered that he dug Manson's ballsiness & style, but wasn't halfway finished when one of the strangers smashed a hidden stone to your friend's temple. You two were not violent, not angry, only loved the rage that shock rock could get out of people, but this rage, their blinding attack was not at authority or ignorance, but at unprocessed trauma, exhaustion from unseen forces.

Two years later was much different. The planes hit when you were in study hall. You were older & more cognizant, but still only seventeen. You turned on the tube after hearing about the first one. Everyone joked about drunk pilots & aliens & the mile-high club. Then the second plane barreled in from the left. No more jokes after that. You looked to your teacher, but she was shaking, holding her hands over her mouth & heart. Unlike Columbine, they kept you in school. Nothing but zombie people. Half-people huddled in corners crying. Dazed teachers trying their best. Most of the school left by lunch. You were at your locker when someone rushing to class tripped & crashed down an entire floor — excruciating screams — whole classrooms flooding out, everyone funneling, rushing to ease any type of pain. That was it. You drove home, turned on the coverage, & ate baby carrots until the blurs of blackness began flipping against the walls of smoke. It was comical at first, & then you realized the blurs were people leaping from the 100th floor of disintegration. You took the TV into your hands & felt the canon change again.

Since 1995, we're not Boomers or X, Millennials or Z—we're a generation of violent communal trauma. Age has nothing to do with Oklahoma City & Columbine & 9/11 & Virginia Tech & Sandy Hook & the Vegas concert & Charleston & Pulse & the Mosque & Synagogue shootings & Parkland & more & more & so many more. Millions of us have grown up with a receptiveness to public unsafety. Accepted fear that comes out in self-harm & bullying, but also, finally, a willing openness to admit our problems & insecurities. Therapy used to be a secret, but now people are celebrating it, & that's oddly thanks to communal trauma. But the numbness, the casualness of entering the second decade of the 21st century & there hardly being a moment of reflection when public mass murder happens, is nauseating. We dissect the murderers, but it's always the same old story of alienation & fear & abandonment. Angry white men. Alone. Pointing fingers. The story we keep telling but doing nothing about. There are fan clubs who claim murdered children are deep-state actors. White supremacists want civil war over delusional visions of cannibalistic pedophile rings in pizza parlors. Holocaust deniers. Because it's much easier to have *that* enemy, one thing to blame. But, I hope, we're better than that. Anger is easy, & we know it's never going to be just one thing—not guns or mental health or race or religion or drugs or fear or trauma or environmental destruction or immigration or taxes or evolving masculinity or language or revenge or privilege or ignorance or a failure of education & welfare & segregation & institutional roadblocks—it's not one thing; it's everything, all of it, all of us, but it's simpler if we have that one thing to blame, any public-square effigy, something we can pick out every day, hit with sticks & say, *I get this pain! I understand this confusion!* Raised hackles, instant defense, when more than anything we need to mourn & learn, publicly, out loud together.

IS YOUR AMERICAN DREAM
out of vogue?

Homeslice was originally written as a theatrical piece. The following pages contain the notes for any staging.

CAST

Any actor can perform any monologue, just as long as the casting doesn't contradict the logistics, i.e., when gender or racial specificity is mentioned. Other than those instances, each monologue (the entire play) is about universal experiences presented in a unique way—that even if the context is different, many of the pieces can resonate and can be performed by any gender, race, or age.

As such, the play can be cast in a multitude of ways: as simple as a solo show or expansive as one actor per monologue, or anything in between.

The *Is Your American Dream—* refrains are recited by the audience, effectively making the audience a chorus and incorporating them into the meaning-making process. This can be accomplished using tech such as projection or screens, or as easy as being printed in the program, or any other creative expression.

TECH

There are no stage directions. This is an invitation to the director/tech director and actor(s) to interpret the script faithfully or to add their own signature.

The production can be a collaboration between the script and (a) visual artist(s)—each monologue paired with (an) onstage visual art interpretation(s). This can be anything: video, sculpture, strategically placed paintings, collage, any creative expression. Similar to casting, it can be accomplished by one artist or many.

Ideally, a single musician or small band performs an impromptu score when inspired, as well as an overture and coda.

Props and costumes are encouraged.

ABOUT THE AUTHOR

DAYTON J. SHAFER's pieces have been featured in fringe festivals, barns, abandoned factories, converted laundromats, black boxes, street sides, and with Vermont Public Radio, the Susan Calza Gallery, Poem-City, and *Split Lip Magazine*. He's a former writing fellow at Vermont Studio Center, managing editor of *Hunger Mountain Literary Journal*, and grant recipient from the Montpelier Public Arts Commission.

COLOPHON

The edition you are holding is the First Edition of this publication.

The handwritten font is set in Hey November, created by Khurasan. The secondary sans-serif title font and the page numbers are set in Avenir Book, created by Adrian Frutiger. The Alternating Current Press logo is set in Portmanteau, created by JLH Fonts. All other text is set in Iowan Old Style, created by John Downer. All fonts used with permission and full commercial license; all rights reserved.

Cover jacket is designed by Leah Angstman. Cover artwork is by Nika Akin. Interior frontispiece illustration is by Josie Colt. Cassette tape illustrations are by Tartila and WinWin ArtLab. The Alternating Current lightbulb logo is created by Leah Angstman, ©2013, 2023 Alternating Current. The Little Pigeon series logos were created by Leah Angstman, ©2020, 2023, Alternating Current. All images used with permission; all rights reserved.

Other Works from
ALTERNATING CURRENT PRESS

All of these books (and more) are available at the
Alternating Current Press website: altcurrentpress.com.

altcurrentpress.com

www.ingramcontent.com/pod-product-compliance
Lightning Source LLC
Chambersburg PA
CBHW030350100526
44592CB00010B/893